Mystery in the Wax Museum: The Magic of Madame Tussaud

By
Herbert Ellis

Illustrated by
Howard Nostrand

cpi
contemporary perspectives, inc.

This book is distributed by Silver Burdett Company, Morristown, New Jersey 07960.

Library of Congress Number: 79-19627

Art and Photo Credits

Cover Illustration by Howard Nostrand.

Photos on pages 4, 9, Culver Pictures, Inc.
Photos on pages 23, 24, 37, 41, 43, 44, 47, and 48, courtesy of Madame Tussaud's, London.
Photo on page 27, courtesy of Musée Carnavalet.
Photo on page 33, Granger Collection, New York.

Every effort has been made to trace the ownership of all copyrighted material in this
book and to obtain permission for its use.

Library of Congress Cataloging in Publication Data

Ellis, Herbert, 1930-
    Mystery in the wax museum: The Magic of Madame Tussaud

    SUMMARY: A biography of the French woman whose
skill at modelling wax figures brought her fame before
and during the French revolution and later in the British
Isles where she eventually settled and established her
famous museum.
    1. Tussaud, Marie, 1761-1850 — Juvenile literature.
2. Wax modellers — France — Biography — Juvenile
literature. [1. Tussaud, Marie, 1761-1850. 2. Wax
modellers] I. Title.
NK9582.T87E43   736'.93'0924 [B]   [92]   79-19627
ISBN 0-89547-084-5

Manufactured in the United States of America
ISBN 0-89547-084-5

Contents

On July 14, 1789 the storming of the Bastille marked the beginning
of the French Revolution.

Setting the Stage

France was a hard place to live in the late 1700s. There seemed to be only two kinds of people in the country. There were the very rich and the very poor. The well-to-do were those who ate every day. Most people, without jobs and penniless, ate when they could.

Those who owned land were grateful to their king. His royal army protected their lands. But those who worked for the landowners did not feel as warmly toward the king. They could not feed their families. They blamed the *royalists* — King Louis XVI and his followers — for taking too much and giving the people too little.

France was ruled by the royalists. To be in government one had to come from the "right" family. The king and his wife, Queen Marie Antoinette, could decide which were the "right" families. As for France's poor, their unhappiness grew.

A war between the royalists and the people was coming. There was no doubt of it. And by the end of 1793, the king and queen had been put to death.

Chapter 1
A Visit to the Cemetery

The dark chill of night hung over the city of Paris. It was October 16, 1793. King Louis had been dead for nine months. The city was once again quiet at night.

But now the sound of voices broke the nighttime stillness. Marie Grosholtz jumped from her bed and ran to the window. She peeked out from behind a curtain. Three soldiers stood at the door. A chill went through Marie. These men wore the uniforms of the revolutionary army. Why would they want to see her uncle in the middle of the night?

Marie heard the door open. From her window she saw her uncle hold up a lantern. The glow lighted the faces of the three soldiers. "Well, what is it this time?" she heard her uncle ask.

One of the men stepped forward. He spoke so quietly that Marie had to strain to hear his words. "Dr. Curtius, again we need you. In the name of the revolution, get your things and come with us. And bring Marie. She will also be needed tonight."

Dr. Curtius shook his head. "No! Marie has not been well. Surely I can do what has to be done."

"The captain orders that you bring Marie! Times are changing in France, doctor. We no longer bow to a king. And we will get rid of every last royalist in the country. Marie is the only one who can record these changes. Through her our war for freedom will never be forgotten by the French people."

Again Dr. Curtius shook his head. "My niece has gone with us before. This time I must say no. Why do you even ask this of her? You know Marie was close to the royal family. Just this afternoon the queen — Marie Antoinette — was put to death. Marie loved this woman very much. All day she has not eaten. She has thought of nothing but the awful blade that cut off the queen's head. Surely you don't now expect . . . ."

"Uncle Philippe, please don't worry about me." Marie's calm, cool voice came from the top of the staircase behind him. "I have everything we will need. Please take this bag. I will get my cloak."

Soon five figures were making their way through the quiet Paris night. The sound of their heels against the cobblestones echoed through the dark, narrow streets. They were heading toward the Cemetery of the Madeleine.

Marie and her uncle almost had to run to keep up with the soldiers. Dr. Curtius watched his niece out of the corner of his eye. She stared straight ahead. It was

Queen Marie Antoinette rode in silence to face death under the awful blade.

as though she were in a trance — half asleep, half awake. Dr. Curtius was worried. Marie was not herself. Would she be able to do what these "butchers" were asking?

Finally the five reached the cemetery. The soldiers swung open the gate. They led Marie and Dr. Curtius to a small house just inside the dark graveyard.

Dr. Curtius needn't have worried about his niece. Marie had been here before. She knew exactly what to do. Without a word, she took the leather bag from her uncle. She set it on a table in the middle of the room.

The only light in the windowless room came from a wall lantern. Long shadows fell on the wall across from the table where Marie worked. First she set out several jars of oil. Then she placed a pouch of plaster on the table. No one in the room spoke.

It was Marie who finally broke the eerie silence. "I will need a bucket of water to mix the plaster."

A young soldier rushed out to get the water. As they waited, Dr. Curtius stepped forward. "Marie, perhaps it would be better if I did this. You are not well."

His niece's eyes were cold and hard. Her uncle was frightened. Marie seemed to be looking right through him. It was as if he were not even in the room. She spoke only three words. "Leave me alone."

Then Marie took the water from the soldier. In the same cold voice she said, "I am ready to begin."

10

Another soldier stepped forward. He placed a bundle on the table in front of Marie. For just a second Dr. Curtius thought he saw Marie's hands tremble. Then she began to work.

Marie removed the cloth that covered the queen's head. She smoothed the hair back away from the face. Not once did the young woman falter. Next she rubbed oil into the dead queen's skin. Working quickly, Marie spread a coat of freshly made plaster across the lifeless features. Now the plaster had to set. This waiting time seemed to be the most difficult for Marie. Dr. Curtius stared at his niece. He saw small beads of perspiration running down her face. And ... was that a tear forming in the corner of her eye?

There was a faraway look on Marie Grosholtz's face. It told Dr. Curtius that only his niece's body was here in this bleak room. Her mind was someplace else. What was the young woman thinking? Was she remembering the happy hours she had spent at Versailles with the royal family? Dr. Curtius suddenly realized he would never again know what this mysterious woman was thinking. No one would. Perhaps others had already felt this way about Marie. There were those, her uncle knew, who said Marie was somehow not quite *human*!

The plaster had dried. Marie removed the mask. A soldier quickly stepped forward and took the head from the table. It could now be buried with the rest of the queen's body. Marie put her bottles and tools back into the leather bag. Dr. Curtius carefully wrapped the hard plaster cast in a clean cloth. Marie's work had only begun. But there was nothing else to do at the cemetery.

Dr. Curtius and Marie Grosholtz walked home alone. The sun was just starting to rise over the River Seine. Paris was beginning to wake up. Yet uncle and niece, walking home on the Boulevard du Temple, were in their own world. Neither one spoke until they reached the front door. Before they went in, Marie turned to her uncle.

"Uncle Philippe, you must promise me never, *never*, to mention this night again. I don't think I could bear to remember what happened tonight. Do you promise?"

Philippe Curtius was amazed by the change that had taken place in Marie. As the sun rose, the young woman seemed to become herself again. This was not the cold, empty woman who had been to the cemetery with him. What could have changed her?

Dr. Curtius placed his arm around Marie's shoulders as he opened the door. "Never, Marie. I swear never to mention this night again."

Chapter 2
Prison

Month after month the long fight against the royalists went on. Marie's uncle, Philippe Curtius, was called away from Paris to serve in the army.

Many more times Marie Grosholtz was taken from her home in the dark of night. There seemed to be no end to the number of royalist heads in the Paris cemeteries. But one night the soldiers came to Marie for quite another reason.

"Marie Grosholtz, you are under arrest. You have been accused of treason against the new government."

One of the soldiers who had come to the door read from an official-looking paper. "Your mother and aunt are also under arrest. They must come with you."

"I am the only one here who was friendly with the royal family. I am accused of treason simply because I knew King Louis and Queen Marie Antoinette. My mother and aunt did not."

"My orders are to imprison the members of this family, and that is exactly what I shall do!" the soldier answered angrily.

Marie saw that her efforts to save her mother and aunt were hopeless. While the soldiers stood guard at the door, Marie woke the older women. They were able to take little with them . . . some warm clothing and a bit of bread. Then they were marched through the streets to the Carmelite Prison.

The three women were put in a small cell with 17 others. Their room was dark and damp. Dirty straw lay heaped around the floor. Each pile of straw was a prisoner's bed for the night.

Marie forced herself to think as clearly as she could. The important thing to do right now, she decided, was to make her mother and aunt as comfortable as possible. She scanned the crowded room. Then she noticed a young woman quite apart from the others. She was sitting alone in the corner. Marie steered her mother and aunt toward the woman.

"There seems to be a little extra room here. May we sit down?" Marie did not wait for an answer, but helped her mother and aunt to the ground.

"You may. But you will be sitting next to a woman whose husband has just had his head cut off. That's why the others stay away from me. They do not wish to be seen talking with me."

Marie sighed as she sat down against the damp wall. "Soon no one in Paris will be able to talk with *anyone* else. We will all be afraid we are committing some crime against the government."

"Well, I am Josephine Beauharnais, and I am happy to talk with you!" replied the woman.

"And I am Marie Grosholtz."

"Ah, yes, I have seen your wax figures. They are truly beautiful . . . that is, those from before the revolution. But the more recent ones — the king and queen and all those loyal to the throne — I . . . I don't understand how you could have done such a thing to them," said Josephine.

Here Marie interrupted. "I, myself, don't understand sometimes. But I did them. And that's that!"

A silence fell between the two women. Marie took a loaf from beneath her cloak. She divided it into four portions. One of these she held out to Josephine Beauharnais. The four women ate quietly.

Three days passed. Once each day the women were given water and bread. Marie passed the time talking with Josphine. The two became good friends. Then on the evening of the third day, a guard came and took Marie from the cell. She was led down a long hall and into a small room. A single chair stood in the middle of the room. Marie was told to sit down.

Marie sat there for what seemed a long while. Suddenly she heard the sound of footsteps in the hall.

Someone was nearing the room. Shortly an old man came in. His cold eyes seemed to bore right through Marie's skin. She felt a chill. "I am the prison barber, and I understand you need a haircut," the old man leered.

Marie's long hair lay in tangled knots on her shoulders. The barber picked up a large pair of scissors. With four giant snips, Marie's curls fell to the floor. There they lay mixed with the hair of many others who had sat in that same chair before her. As she was led from the room, the cruel barber caught her by the arm. He leaned over and whispered in her ear. "And tomorrow, Marie? Who will do *your* lovely head in wax?"

When she returned to the cell, the other women gasped in horror. They understood why Marie's hair had been cut away. Marie had taken her first step toward the guillotine — the razor-sharp blade that would remove her head. Tomorrow would certainly be the day.

Marie sat down on the floor in her corner of the room. To the others this young woman was amazing. She seemed completely unafraid. Perhaps the stories about Marie Grosholtz had been true. Perhaps this woman was *not* quite human. How else could she carve those lifelike heads with the look of real flesh? How else could she stay so calm in the very face of death?

Marie heard none of the talk buzzing about her. She was tired. Soon she was fast asleep....

Chapter 3
A Young Girl in Paris

... And Marie was soon dreaming. It was 1767 again. Marie, then a young girl of seven, was coming to Paris. There she would live with her uncle, Dr. Philippe Curtius.

Uncle Philippe had been living in Paris for several years. He no longer practiced medicine. His old hobby was now his full-time job. He shaped the figures of rich people out of wax. Dr. Curtius had done very well selling his wax statues.

The carriage came to a sudden stop in the Rue St. Honoré. Marie jumped down and hurried up the steps of a large house. She had not seen Uncle Philippe in so long! She pounded and pounded on the door. The door finally opened, and she ran past a servant and into the house. Marie ran to look for Uncle Philippe.

The hall was dark. The house seemed so quiet after the noisy Paris streets. She rushed into a large room. The curtains were drawn. No, there was no one here. Then she saw a man standing near the window.

"Uncle Philippe! We're here!" shouted Marie as she rushed across the room. She threw her arms around him. As she did, the figure suddenly toppled to the floor. The head fell off and rolled across the room.

The noise of the crashing figure brought a servant, her mother, and finally her Uncle Philippe running into the room. The servant quickly opened the curtains. Only then did Marie see that she was surrounded by silent wax statues.

"Marie! I'm sure that the Prince de Conti is not quite ready to have his body separated from his head," said her uncle with a smile. "But don't worry child, I'm sure he will forgive you."

By now Marie was no longer afraid. After greeting her uncle she began to study the wax figures that surrounded her. "Uncle Philippe, how real they are! They seem almost alive! How do you make them?" Dr. Curtius was happy that his niece was so interested in his work.

Marie Grosholtz would remember her early years in Paris with Uncle Philippe as the happiest time in her life. It wasn't long after she arrived that her uncle knew that Marie was more than just interested in his work. It became clear that she was also a talented artist. In fact she was becoming far better with the wax than her uncle.

Uncle Philippe taught his young niece all the things he did to make a wax figure. First a person's face was oiled, and the hair was carefully smoothed back. Then plaster was placed on the face. Two tiny holes were made at the nostrils so the person could breathe. When the plaster mask had hardened, it was removed.

Next a clay form was made from the plaster mask. Onto the clay form Marie and her uncle would carefully sculpture every feature and line on a person's face. Another plaster mold was then made from the clay form. Finally, from this last plaster mold the wax figure was made.

Now the skills of a true artist were necessary. The wax figure had to be carefully painted with lifelike colors. Hair had to be inserted into the head. Glass eyes that exactly matched the color and size of the model's were made and set in place.

As wax figures became more popular, Dr. Curtius opened a museum where people could see the wax portraits of the most important people of the day. Many of Marie's wax figures appeared in the museum. The years passed, and Marie's fame grew. Then in 1780 Princess Elizabeth, King Louis XVI's sister, visited Dr. Curtius's museum.

The princess wanted to learn everything there was to know about making wax figures. Would Marie come and live at Versailles as her art teacher? Dr. Curtius was honored. Here was the chance for his niece to live among royalty — in one of the most beautiful palaces in the world.

Making a wax figure is a lot of work. 1.A metal frame, or *armature*, is made. 2.Hot wax and plaster are used to mold the head and body. 3.Glass eyes ▶ are put in place. 4.Hair is inserted into the wax head strand by strand.

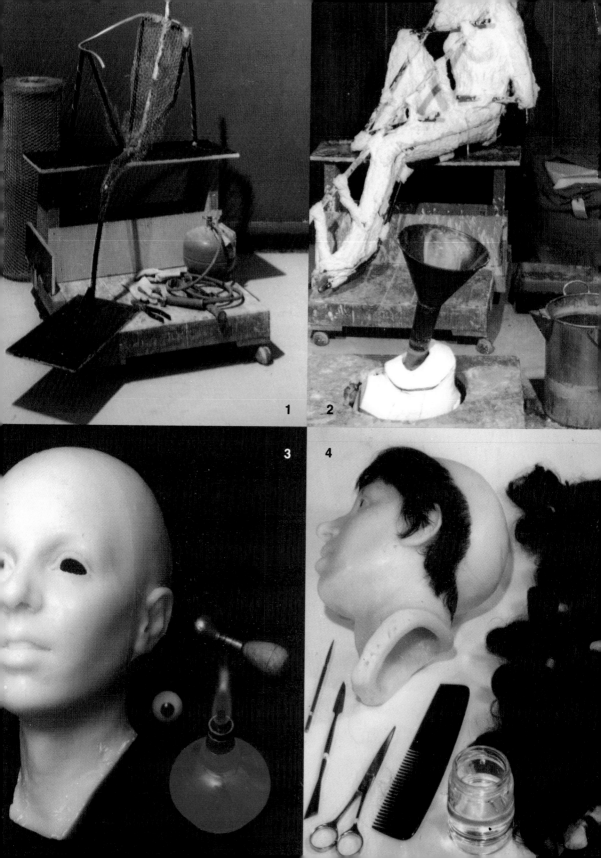

1

2

3

4

For several years Marie Grosholtz lived with the royal family at Versailles. She was surrounded by riches and splendor all week. On weekends she would return to her uncle's home in Paris.

Each weekend she would meet the most important and famous people of Paris. They gathered in Uncle Philippe's living room to talk politics. The talk Marie heard frightened her. Uncle Philippe's friends spoke about a revolution. Many felt that Louis XVI was a bad king who was doing nothing to help his people. While King Louis lived in his beautiful palace, many of his people could not afford to buy even a loaf of bread.

Marie was torn between her love for her uncle and her feelings for King Louis XVI, Queen Marie Antoinette, and their children.

Those who gathered at Uncle Philippe's house wanted a new form of government.

During a visit home in the spring of 1786, Dr. Curtius told Marie he wanted her to leave the palace and come home. "I know that you are very close to Princess Elizabeth and her family," he said. "But I don't think you are safe there. We will soon have a war against the royalists. The king may not survive."

Marie was torn between her love for her uncle and her feelings for the royal family. She knew that something had to be done for the poor people of France, but would war really help anyone? Sadly she packed her bags and said goodbye to her friends at Versailles. Marie moved back to her uncle's house in Paris. The happiest years of her life were over. The terrible years were just beginning.

Back in her uncle's house, Marie was now meeting the very people who would lead the French Revolution. She met Jacques Necker, the Director of Finance. He was desperately trying to save France from ruin. She met the Duke of Orléans, a noble who believed in the equality of all men. Marie met Mirabeau, Danton, Marat, and Robespierre. Each of these famous men would make his mark in bringing about the end of the French throne.

By the summer of 1789 Paris had grown restless. Feelings against the king were growing stronger by the day. Then a rumor spread throughout the city. The king had dismissed Jacques Necker, and the Duke of Orléans had been sent into exile. The people of Paris were outraged. The king, they felt, had no right to treat two of France's most popular citizens in this way.

On Sunday, July 12, a noisy crowd gathered in front of Dr. Curtius's house. From the studio where she worked, Marie could hear their angry shouts: "We want Necker! We want the Duke! We want Necker! We want the Duke!"

At first Philippe Curtius tried to ignore the angry mob. But he soon realized they would not leave until they got what they had come for. Many of the rioters had been to Dr. Curtius's museum. There they had seen the wax figures of Jacques Necker and the Duke of Orléans. Now the crowd wanted to carry the statues of these two heroes through the streets. There was nothing Dr. Curtius could do but turn over the wax figures to the crowd. Marie watched from an upstairs window as they carried off two of the first wax figures she had ever done.

That July day marked the beginning of the French Revolution. In the three years that followed, many people were imprisoned. Many others died on the guillotine. Marie Grosholtz, the most famous wax artist in Paris, was ordered to make wax portraits from their severed heads. Marie had known many of them

Crowds rallied around the wax heads of Necker and the Duke of Orléans.

personally. She had lived with them for years. There was King Louis, Queen Marie Antoinette, and many of the men who had gathered at Philippe Curtius's house. So many were already gone. How much longer would the revolution go on?

Marie now tossed as she slept on the prison floor.

". . . I must get away . . . away from France . . . away from the revolution . . . away from the guillotine. . . ."

Chapter 4
Goodbye to Paris

Marie suddenly awoke from her dream. As she opened her eyes, a man was leaning over her whispering in her ear.

"Hurry! Wake your mother and aunt, and follow me." Marie tried to see the man's face, but he wore a high scarf and his hat was pulled low, hiding his face.

The rest of the women in the cell were fast asleep as the three tiptoed out. In a few minutes Marie, her mother, and her aunt followed the man through the prison gate. A carriage was waiting. The man held the door open and pulled the women in.

The man tipped his hat to Marie. It was Uncle Philippe!

"When I returned to Paris and the three of you were gone, I was frantic. Then I learned that you had been taken to prison. I came as quickly as I could," said Curtius. "Thank heavens I still have friends in the new government!"

Looking at Marie's short hair, he added. "And I see that I got here none too soon."

Marie's stay in prison had been brief. But it had a lasting effect on her. Philippe Curtius watched his niece become an even quieter person. She hardly ever spent time with the rest of the family. Every waking hour of her day was passed in the art studio working on wax portraits. Marie seemed to have hardened.

Time went by, but the revolution seemed never to end. Each month brought a new struggle among the antiroyalists for control of the government. Philippe Curtius tried not to take sides in the struggle. He knew how to stay in business. He made sure that *all* the most popular political figures were in his museum.

Then in September 1794 Philippe Curtius suddenly died. He left Marie his museum and his home.

Marie felt quite alone without her uncle. She now had one aim in life. With no one to protect her, she would have to protect herself. She would survive the war as her Uncle Philippe had survived. She would work to keep her museum one of the most popular places in Paris.

One day Marie learned that Fouquier-Tinville, the bloodthirsty public prosecutor who had guillotined so many Frenchmen, was himself to be guillotined. To Marie this was an opportunity to attract hundreds of people to the museum. For the first time in her life, Marie *asked* to make a death mask of someone who was to be killed. She made the mask, and soon the frightening figure of Fouquier-Tinville was on display at the museum.

Thousands of people flocked to see the figure. Many gasped in horror. The sight of this feared killer — even as a wax statue — was too much for them. But a few who saw the statue came away with a feeling that was more than simple fright. What they had seen was no mere statue, they said. The wax figure seemed to be alive. One man claimed he felt a heartbeat beneath the cloak draped over Fouquier-Tinville's shoulders. A woman swore she saw a tear in the statue's eye.

Rumors raced through Paris. *Marie's new statue had actually started to bleed . . . the arms had reached out to grab a visitor in the museum . . . the statue had a living heart and a mind of its own . . . Marie Grosholtz had somehow brought an evil killer back to life as a piece of wax!*

No human could create life from wax! If Marie Grosholtz was not human, what was she?

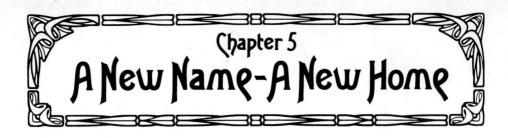

Chapter 5
A New Name-A New Home

In 1795, a year after her uncle's death, Marie Grosholtz married a young engineer. Her new husband was François Tussaud. Marie Grosholtz now took on a new name. She became Madame Tussaud. It is by that name that she became famous throughout the world.

Marie and François worked together to make the museum a success. And they had two sons, Joseph and François. Marie's life was full — and it was busier than ever. As Madame Tussaud she was not at all bothered by what people were saying about the old Marie Grosholtz. Her new family life quieted people's fears about Marie. At least it did for a while.

Then one day Madame Tussaud received a note from the Palace in the Tuileries. The letter was signed by Josephine Bonaparte. This was the wife of France's new leader — Napoleon Bonaparte. Josephine Bonaparte, it seems, was Josephine Beauharnais before she married the new emperor of France. Marie remembered the woman right away. She had shared a cell with her in the Carmelite Prison.

Josephine asked Madame Tussaud to come to the palace. She wanted Marie to do a wax portrait of her husband, Napoleon.

The leaders of the revolution thought France would never again be ruled by a monarch. But in 1804 Napolean Bonaparte made himself emperor of France.

In 1796 Napoleon had been made the First Consul of France. It was, of course, an honor to be asked to do a wax figure of the man. It was also a good deal of trouble. He was always busy with the details of government. Josephine finally convinced him to take the time to have his portrait done by Madame Tussaud. She finally got an appointment with him to make her wax mold. It was for five o'clock in the morning!

Josephine was delighted to see Marie again. They had not met since their days in prison. Josephine brought Marie into a room where Napoleon impatiently waited. They were introduced. Napoleon grumbled an abrupt "Hello."

Marie began. She worked quickly and confidently. Napoleon was restless. When Marie prepared to smear plaster all over his face, the great warrior looked alarmed.

"Don't worry. This won't hurt," said Marie.

Embarrassed, Napoleon shot his answer back at her. "Worry! Me? I wouldn't worry if you pointed 20 loaded pistols at my head!" And that may have been true. The fiery French leader was certainly said to be brave. But he had also heard a great deal about Madame Tussaud from his wife. She had told him of Marie's calm escape from certain death under the blade. From others Napoleon had heard of the mysterious powers of this woman who could turn wax figures into "living" beings. Napoleon laughed loudly when he heard such talk. Of course he didn't believe a

34

word of it. But his own wife, Josephine, was not quite sure why he seemed so nervous around Madame Tussaud.

When the mold was made, Josephine took Marie to one side. "Please be especially careful with his wax portrait," she whispered. "I'm sure I could never get him to let you do another one."

How many times had Napoleon seen Madame Tussaud's lifelike wax people with his own eyes? He needed no one to make him wonder about this mysterious woman. He already wondered about her. *Why had so many of the people she had done in wax later lost their heads?* There in her museum one could see royalists and antiroyalists she had shaped before and *after* their deaths.

How had this woman, herself almost a part of the royal family, escaped death? Her uncle had been the friend of antiroyalists. She had lived with the king's own family. How had she not been killed by one side or the other?

Why did only Madame Tussaud's wax statues seem to "glow" with life? Others had done wax figures before. Her own uncle had done them. Yet of all the wax work in Europe, people were shaken only by the figures and faces shaped by Madame Tussaud. Why? ... Why?

If Napoleon was truly upset by Madame Tussaud, there was certainly no sign of his worry when he saw his face in wax. Madame Tussaud didn't realize how successful she had been with Napoleon until several weeks later. Two of Napoleon's top generals arrived at her studio one morning. Both were dressed in their brightest uniforms. Napoleon, having seen his own wax portrait, had sent them to Madame Tussaud so that she might also do their portraits.

Once again Madame Tussaud had won! The most respected person in France had paid her his greatest honor. Royalty and the enemies of royalty had all bowed to her. And now she had the admiration of the greatest general of all time. The world, one would think, belonged to this talented, brave woman. But no. This was not to be.

Madame Tussaud — Marie Grosholtz — would remain a woman of mystery right to the end.

In 1802 Madame Tussaud suddenly decided to pack up her best 36 figures and take them to England. She also took her son, Joseph, with her.

When she left France she carried her secrets with her. None of those who had known her — those who loved or feared her talents — would ever have the answers they so much wanted. Even Napoleon, by now the strongest ruler in Europe, would never know the "secrets of life" so many thought belonged to Madame Tussaud.

With four-year-old Joseph, she crossed the English Channel. As far as anyone knows, she never again returned to France. A part of her life seemed to have ended. A new part began.

While Napoleon swept through Italy fighting the Austrians, Marie Tussaud began traveling throughout Ireland and Scotland. She carried with her the small exhibit she had brought from France. Then she settled in London. It was here that she opened Madame Tussaud's Wax Museum.

Most people who visit the city of London make it a point to look in on Madame Tussaud's Wax Museum. Although Marie Tussaud died in 1850, her son and family spent their lives continuing to build the museum.

Visitors in London flocked to Madame Tussaud's Exhibition in 1884.

Yet while new statues have been placed in the museum every year, the most interesting figures are still the oldest ones — the ones done by Madame Marie Tussaud. Most people say they are the most lifelike, the most frightening — the best.

Perhaps it is just that wax figures are no longer made the way they were in Marie's time. Today wax figures are not always made from actual masks molded to a real face. The figures are made from photographs.

Or perhaps there really is some truth to the idea that these statues by Marie Tussaud do have some special "glow of life" inside them. Could this be why not a single wax figure was lost or destroyed as they were carried from France to England? Despite all of the bombs dropped on London during World War II, Madame Tussaud's "living" wax still lives to frighten and amaze the museum's visitors.

And speaking of scaring visitors, there is another question to answer before we can call Marie's "living" wax a lot of nonsense.

Could *you* spend the night, all by yourself, with Madame Tussaud's wax figures from olden-day France? As far as we know, *no one* ever has. Even the people who work there like to clear out as early as possible. Some say that "strange things" go on there when it gets dark.

Take the case of young Craig Thompson. . . .

Chapter 6
A Night Visitor

On a cold winter night in 1977, Craig Thompson, a young attendant, was closing Madame Tussaud's Wax Museum for the night. All of the visitors had gone. The lights had been dimmed. An eerie glow came from the rooms where the silent wax figures stood. Craig was finishing the first day of his new job at the museum.

I'll just make sure the back door is locked once more, Craig thought. I wouldn't want to forget anything on my first day.

As he walked through the museum's rooms, the only sound he heard was the clanging of the large keys that hung from his belt. But suddenly he thought he heard a voice.

"Excuse me, young man, but there are several people in here I don't know. Could you tell me a little about them?"

Craig turned quickly. The unexpected voice had scared him. He had thought he was alone in the museum. There in the shadows stood a little old lady. She was dressed in black and she wore an odd-looking bonnet with a white ruffle and a big bow that tied under her chin. Her dress reached to the floor. Her sleeves were long and puffed. Bright, shining eyes peeked out at him from behind her small steel-rimmed glasses.

"There is certainly no reason to be afraid," thought Craig. "Why am I shaking so?"

"I'm sorry, madam, but the museum is closed for the night. I'll take you to the door."

The old lady ignored what he was saying. It was as if he had never spoken. She turned back into the room. "This young woman with the short hair. Who is she? That black suit she is wearing isn't what all the girls are wearing these days, is it?"

Craig shrugged. Oh well, here is the chance to see what I know about some of the figures, he thought to himself. It won't hurt to spend a few minutes here at the museum. I think the others were only trying to scare me with those strange stories about this place at night. The woman's voice interrupted Craig's thoughts.

"Well, young man, who is she?" the little old lady asked again.

"That is Liza Minelli. She's an American singer and movie star. She's pretty popular here in England too," replied Craig.

Is this really Liza Minelli, or is it her wax portrait? You can ▶ see for yourself at Madame Tussaud's Wax Museum!

"Movie star? Well, don't bother to explain. Things sure have changed since my day. A woman wearing pants!" The old woman shook her head.

The little old lady moved across the room to the spot where an elderly figure sat. Close by stood the figure of a plump man.

"I don't believe I recognize these people either," said the woman.

"That gentleman is Alfred Hitchcock. He has made some of the scariest movies ever," Craig explained.

"Movies again. Well, I don't know anything about movies, but I could tell you a scary story or two," replied the woman.

Craig continued. "The woman seated below Mr. Hitchcock is Dame Agatha Christie. She has written many murder mystery stories."

"She looks like the kind of person I would like to know. We would have a lot to talk about," said the little old lady.

The next room the woman wandered into was the Grand Hall. Craig followed closely behind her.

"Here we have all our figures of British royalty," explained Craig.

42   Marie Tussaud would have strange stories of her own ▶
          to tell to Alfred Hitchcock and Dame Agatha Christie.

"Yes, yes, I *do* recognize some of the figures in here. Why, there's Henry VIII and his six wives. Queen Elizabeth I is over there. I know many others too," said the old woman as she wandered through the room.

"Young man, I would like to visit just one more room before I leave. Where is the Separate Room?" she asked.

Craig had never heard that name before. "I'm sorry, but we don't have an exhibition called the Separate Room," he replied.

England's King Henry VIII and his six wives seem to live again through the mysterious "magic" of the wax artist.

"Well, then I guess they are still calling it the Chamber of Horrors. I never did like that name," answered the woman.

"Yes, we do have a room called the Chamber of Horrors. Some of our oldest figures are there. The ones done by Madame Tussaud herself stand in that room. The death masks Madame did of French revolutionary figures are still some of the most popular ones we have."

The little old lady spent a long time in the Chamber of Horrors. She studied each figure carefully. For a while she stood in front of the terrible guillotine.

"Yes, I can see why this room is so popular. Even if I say so myself, some of the figures in here are the best in the exhibit. I'm sure that many people come to see the murderers and criminals who are here. I like the figures from the French Revolution best."

Craig turned to the door. "I'm afraid I must lock up now. You can come back any time during regular visiting hours," he said.

The little old lady smiled. "I don't think I'll be back this way for a long time to come. But thank you for your kindness in letting me see the museum."

As the two headed for the door, the large figure of a black man in a white robe and boxing gloves caught the old lady's eye. She stopped for a minute and looked up at the wax figure of Muhammad Ali. "I've never seen anyone like him before. He is the *greatest*!" exclaimed the woman.

Craig laughed as he opened the door. The little old lady slipped out. Maybe this woman wasn't so crazy after all, Craig thought.

He turned to close the door behind him. As he did so, the wax figure of Madame Tussaud that sits at the entrance to the museum caught his eye. She was dressed all in black. She had an odd-looking bonnet with a white ruffle and a big bow that tied under her chin. Her dress reached to the floor. Her sleeves were long and puffed. Bright, shining eyes peeked out at him from behind her small steel-rimmed glasses.

Craig scratched his head. He started to walk back into the museum, but stopped short. Suddenly it seemed like a good time to leave. He slipped out the front door and locked the bolt behind him. What about those strange stories he had heard about the museum's secret nighttime "life"? No, Craig said to himself, I will think of that some other day!

He had done his job well. Madame Tussaud's wax figures would be safe now. The museum fell silent, the

Sports fans around the world know ▶
Muhammad Ali as "the Greatest."

The wax figure of Madame Tussaud watches over her creations at the museum in London.

figures hidden by darkness. But the morning would bring new visitors to share their mysteries and to wonder at the grand art of Madame Tussaud.